For curious minds and bright hearts, who find joy in art and imagination. May each stroke of these pages be a journey, and each color be a unique expression of the magical world that only you, little artists, can create. May this coloring book be the beginning of many colorful adventures and artistic discoveries. Lovingly dedicated to all the children who make each page special with their unique creativity

Andre Rocha

2023

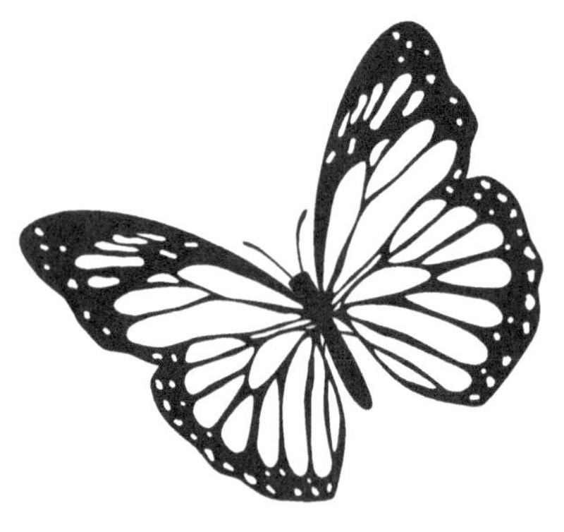

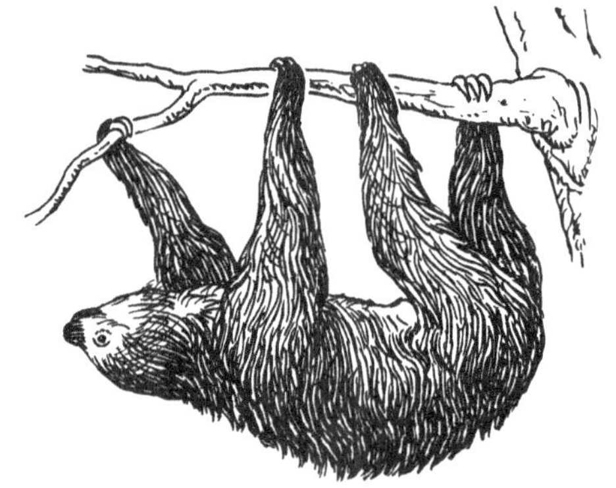

This Book Belongs to:

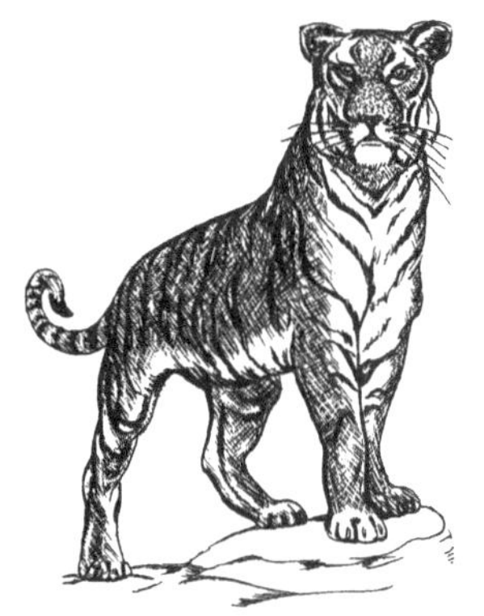

Andre Rocha
2023

Test Color Page

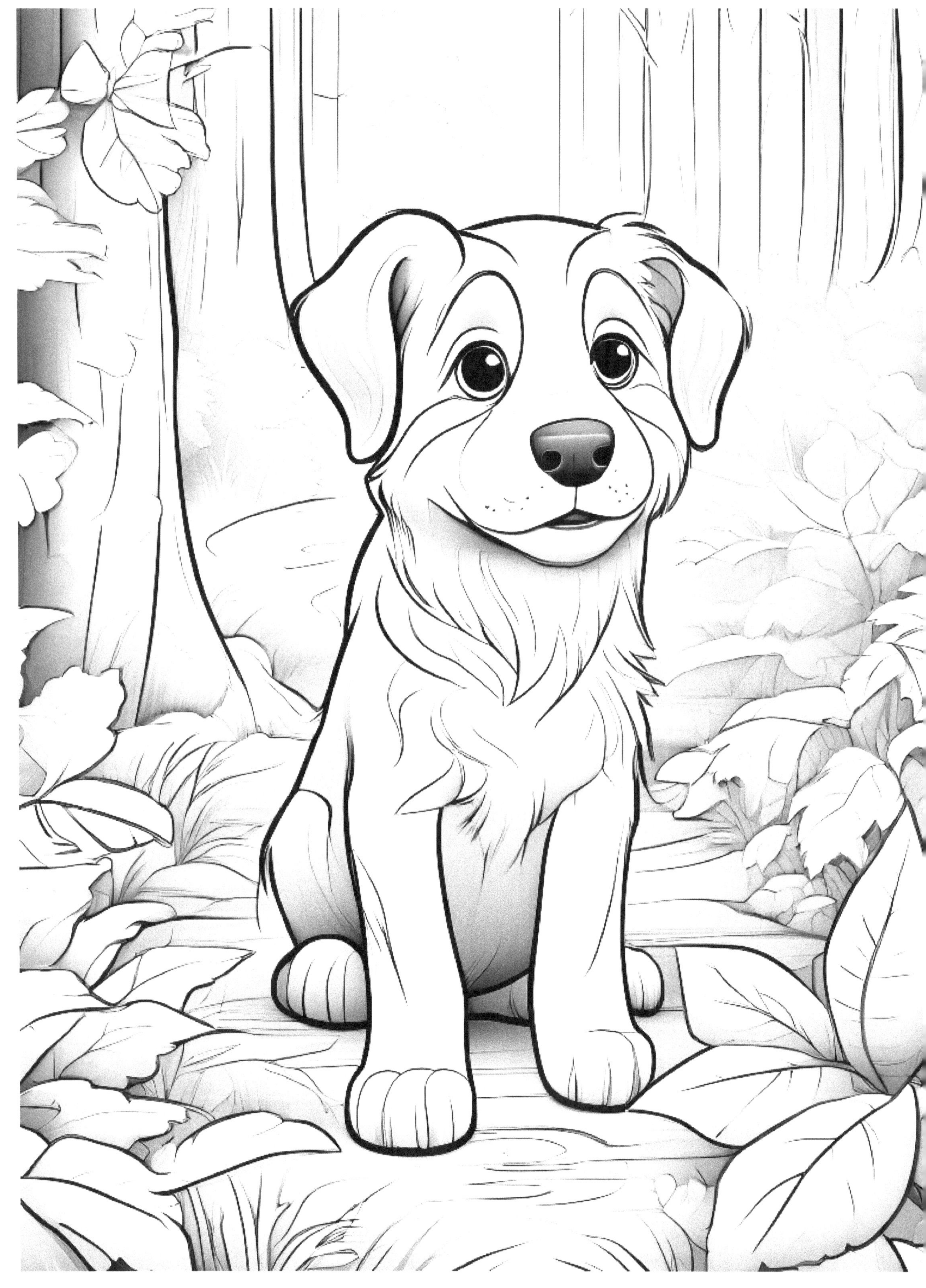

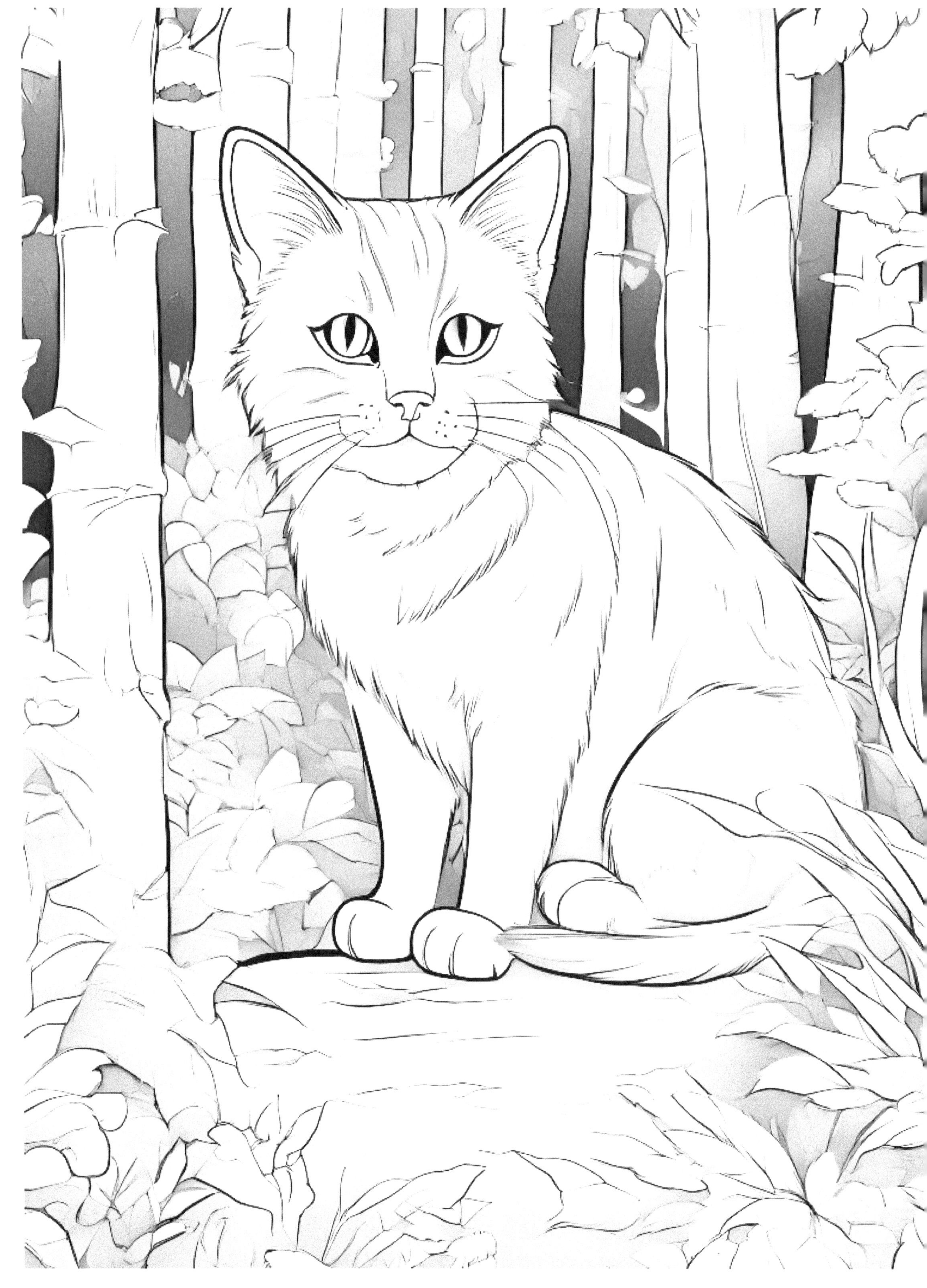

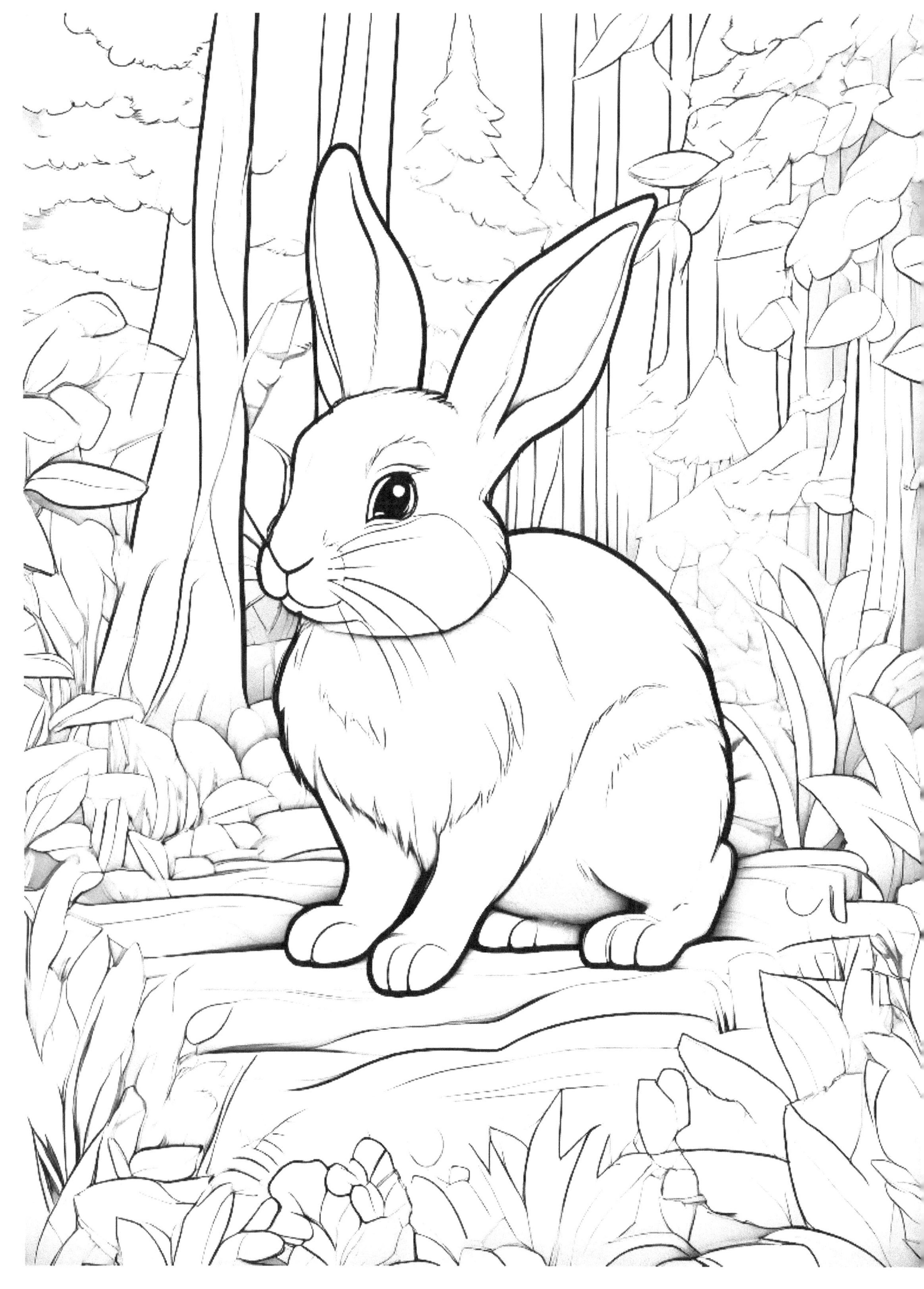

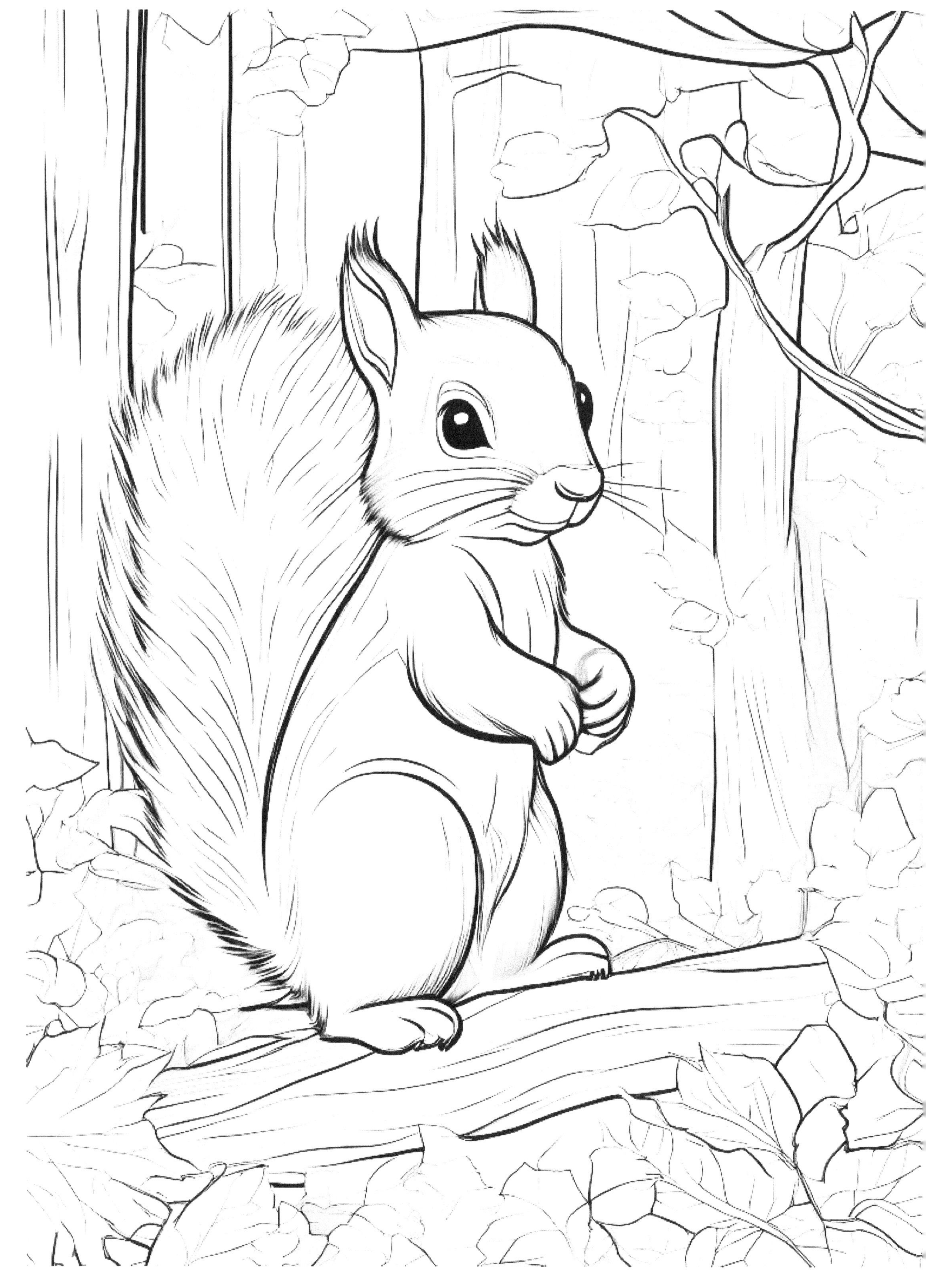

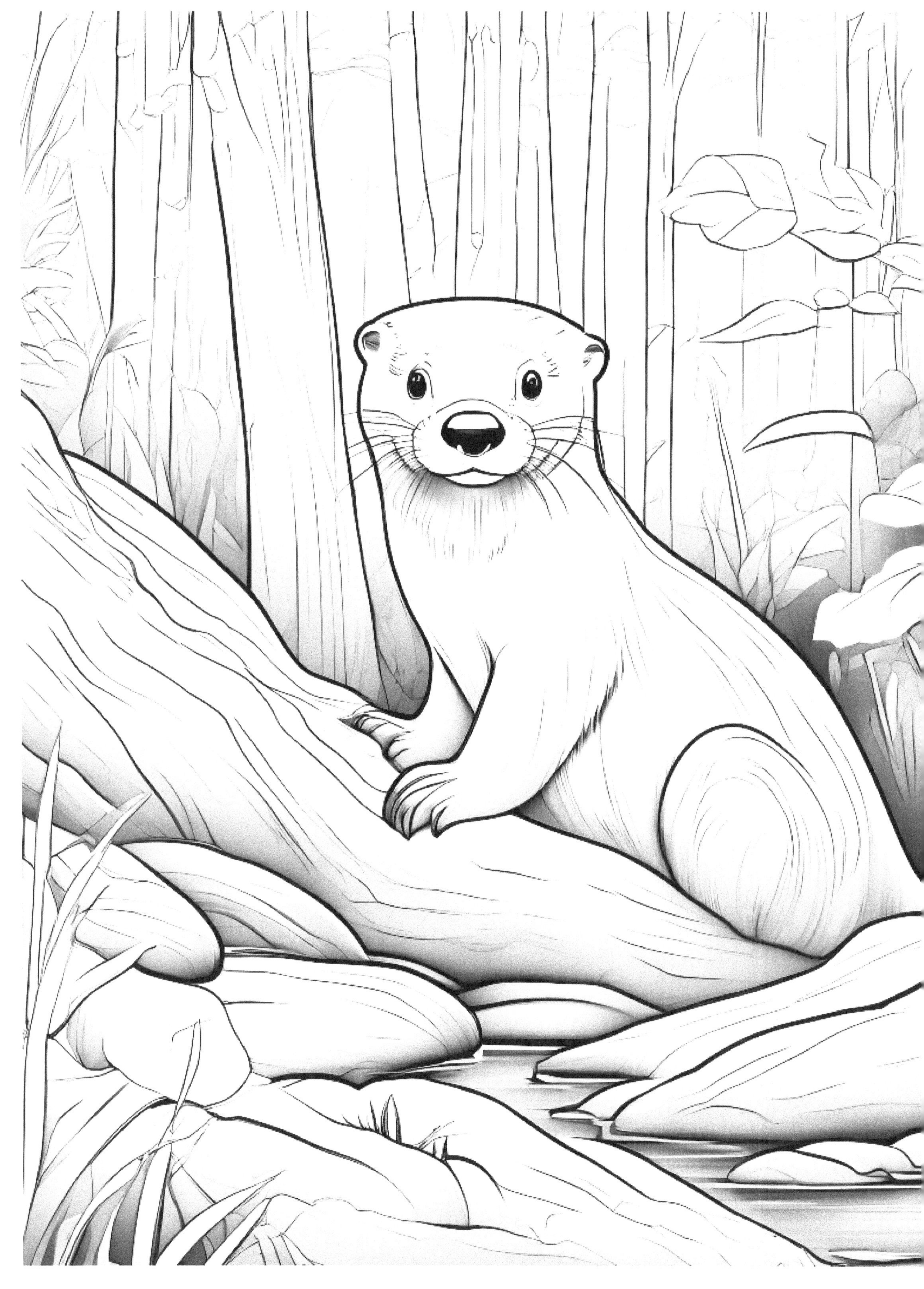

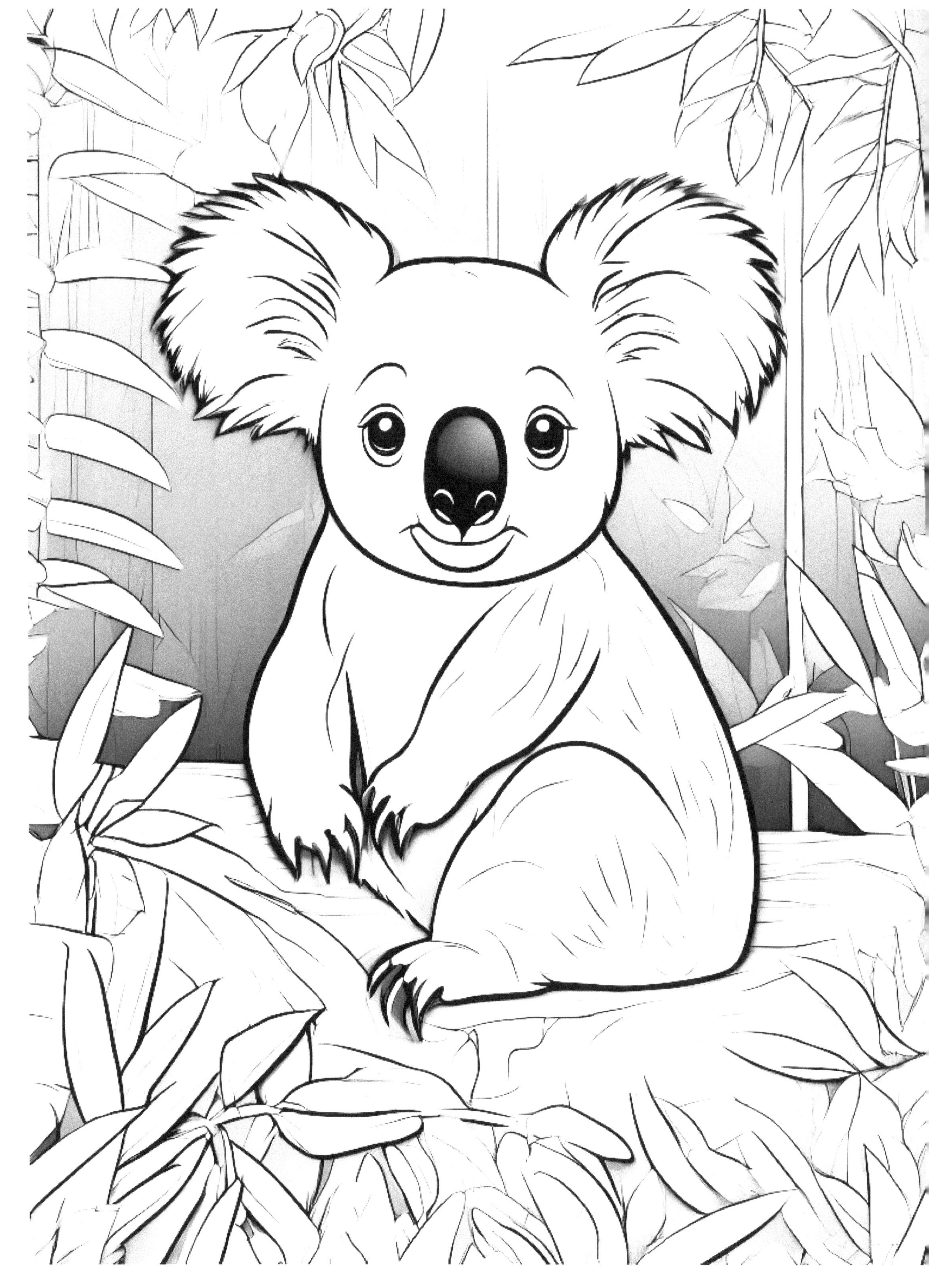

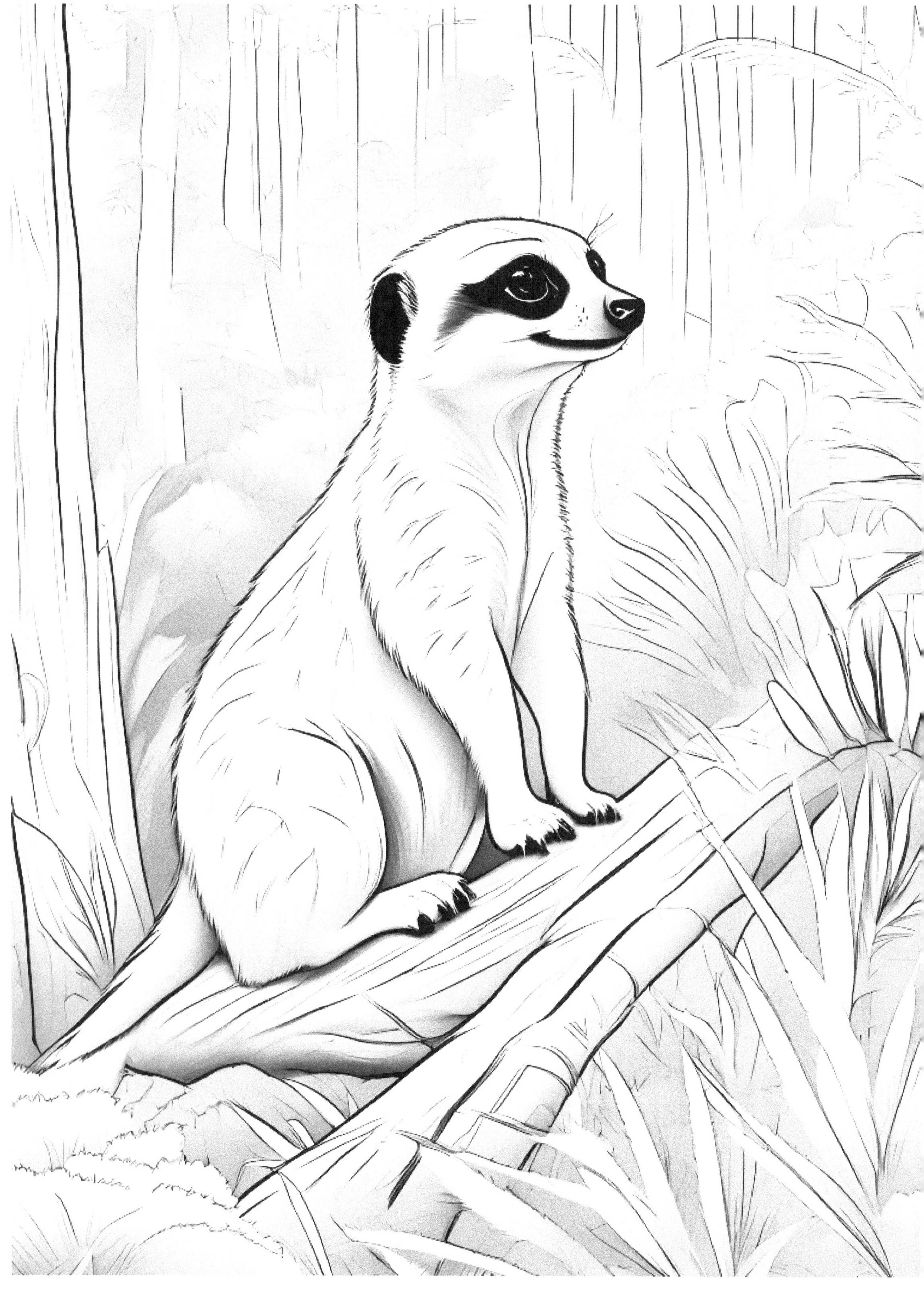

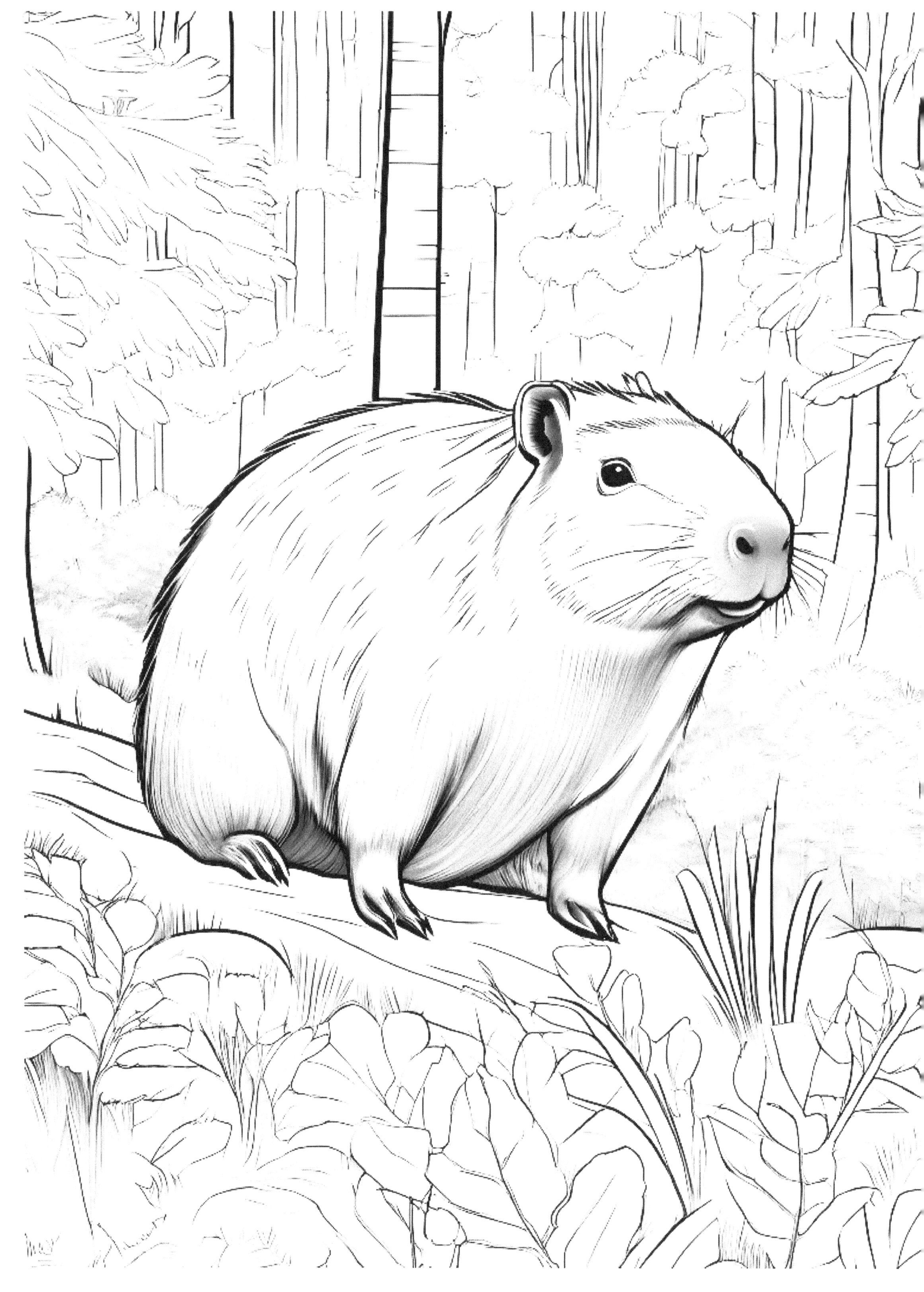

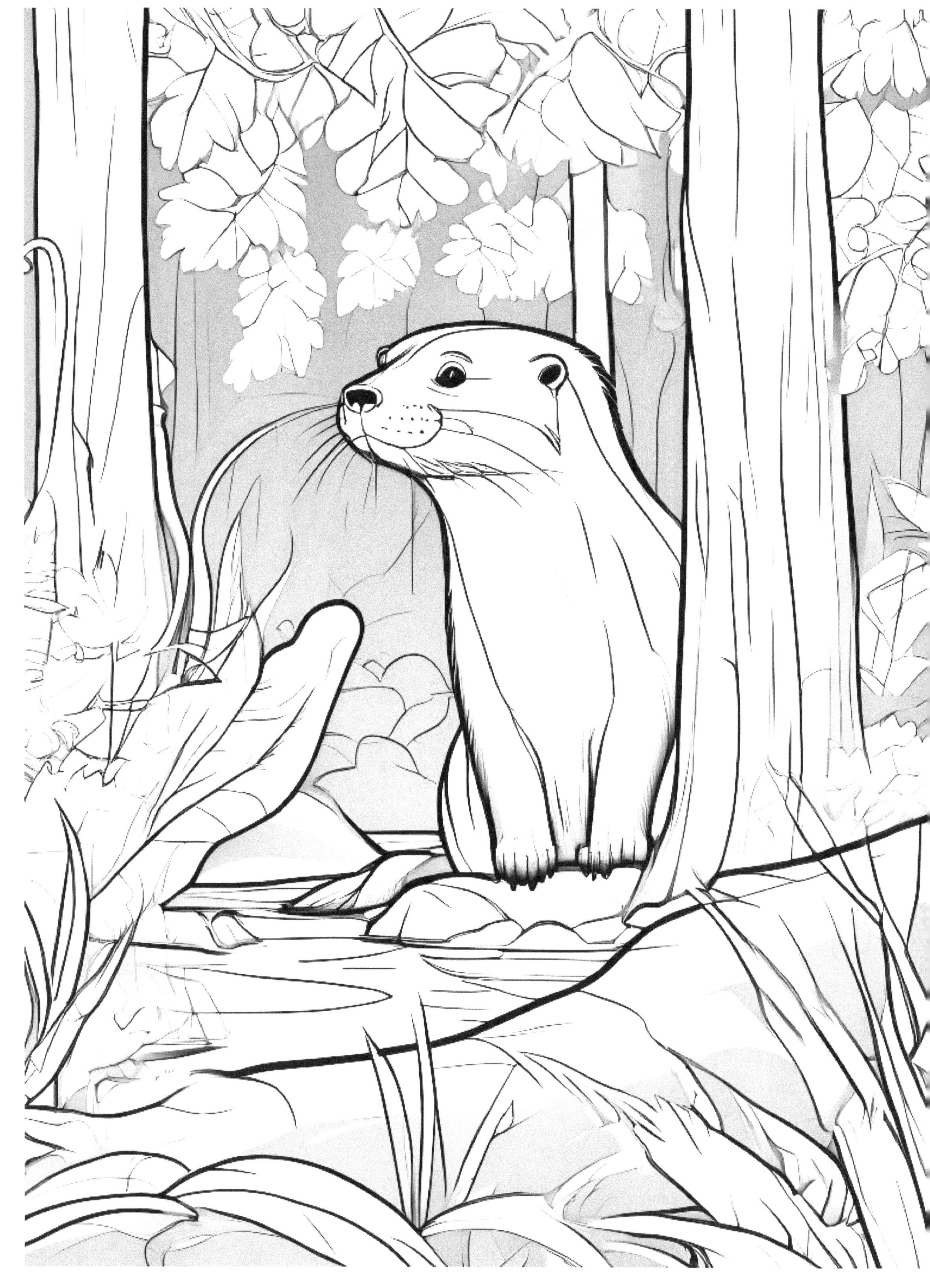

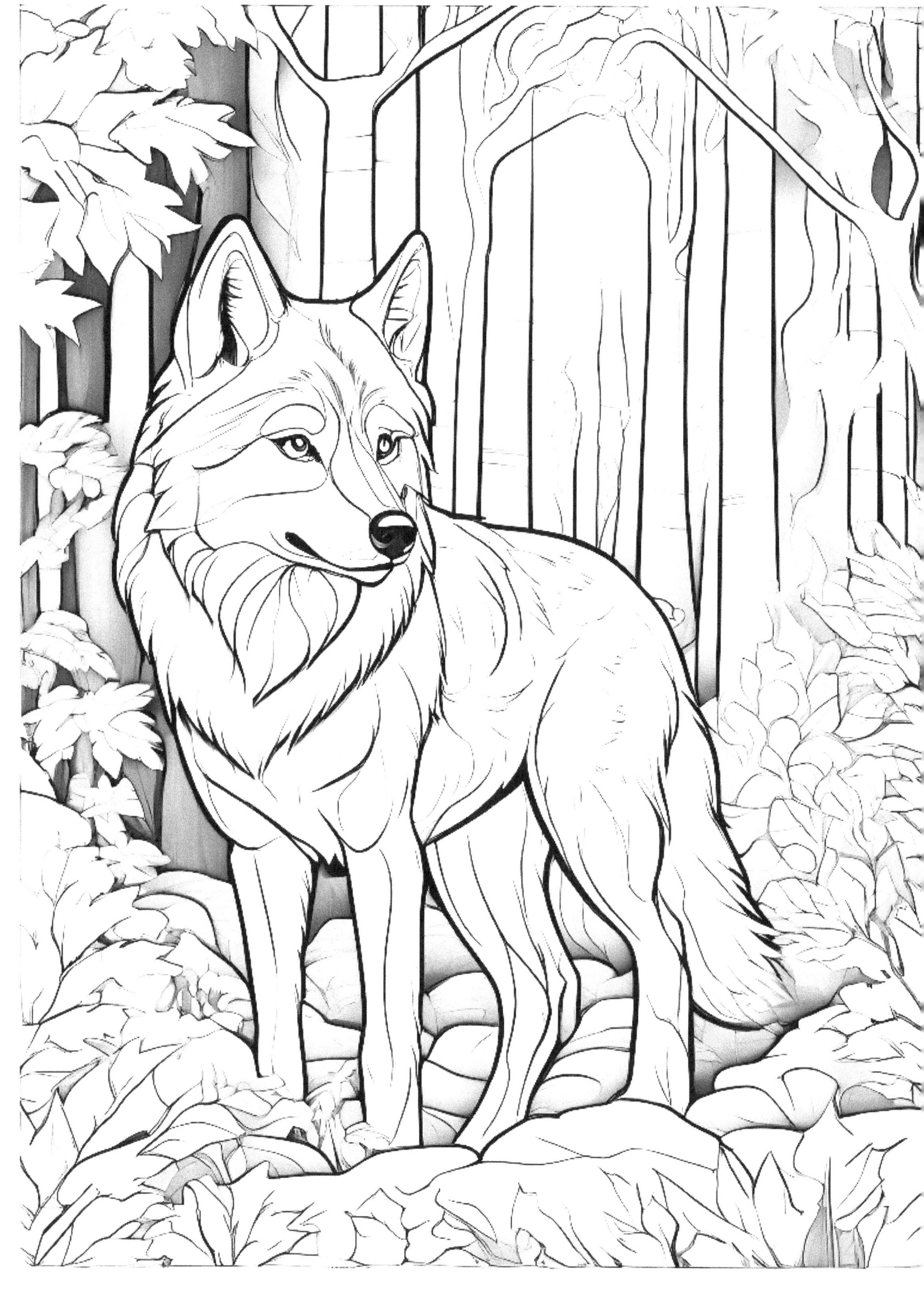

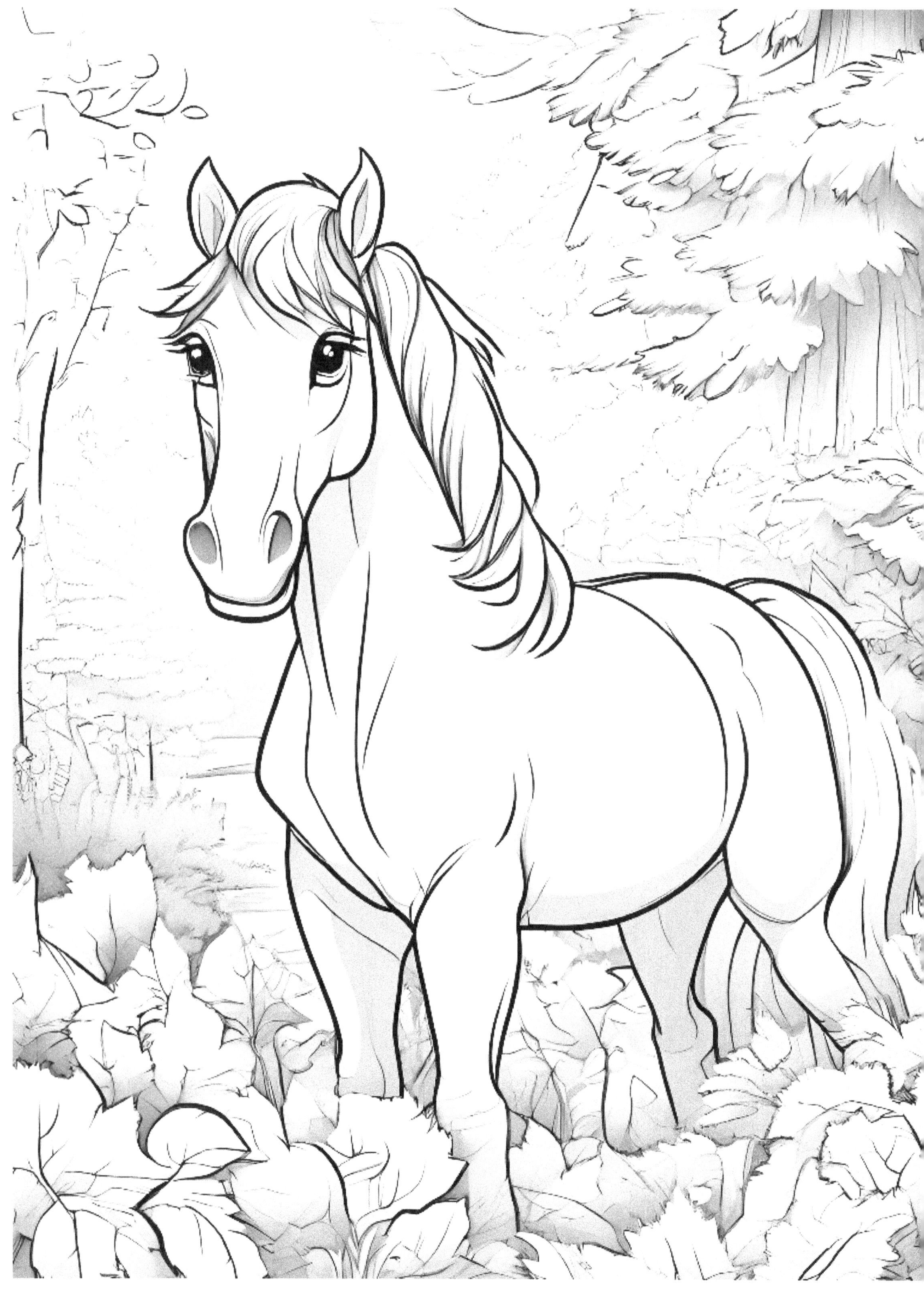

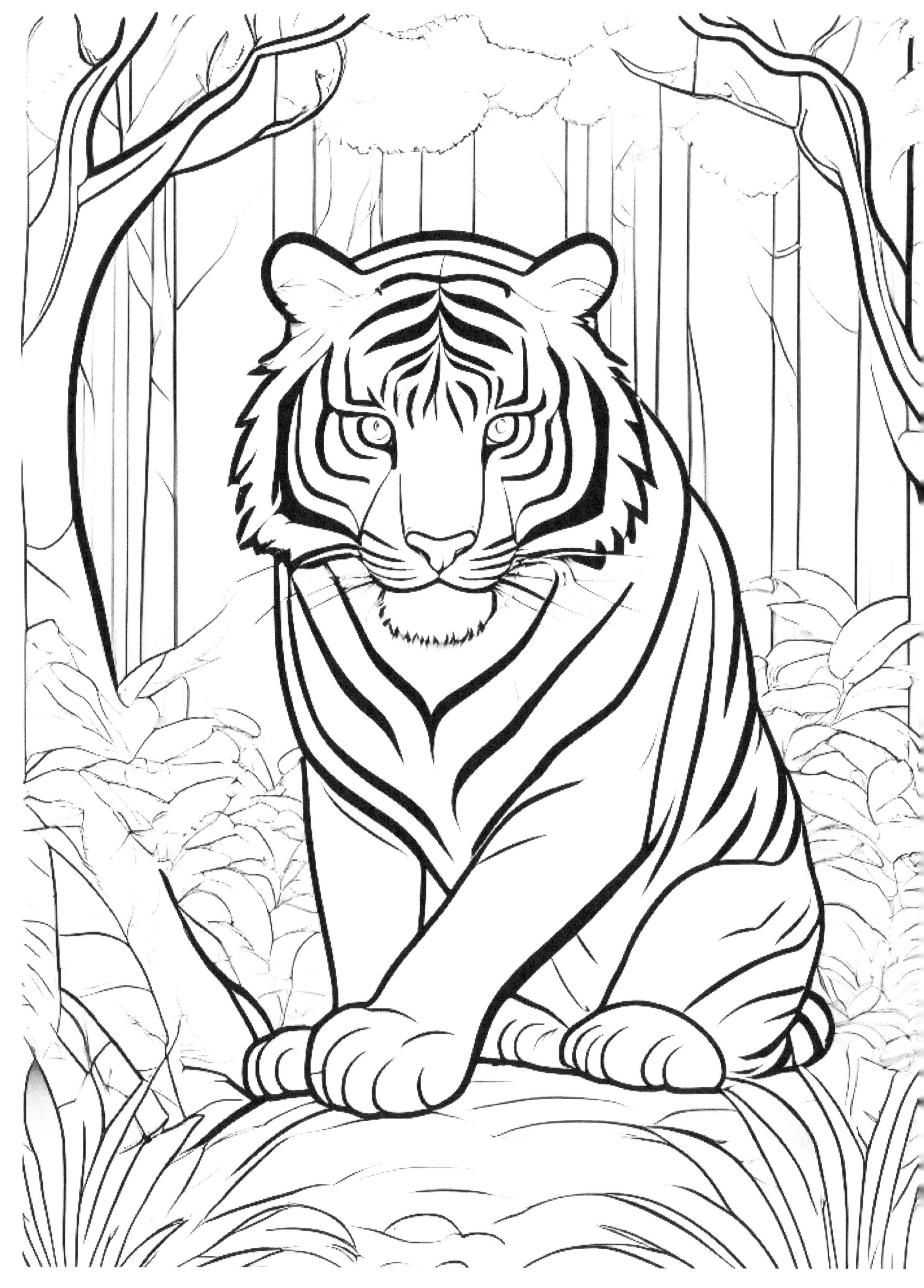

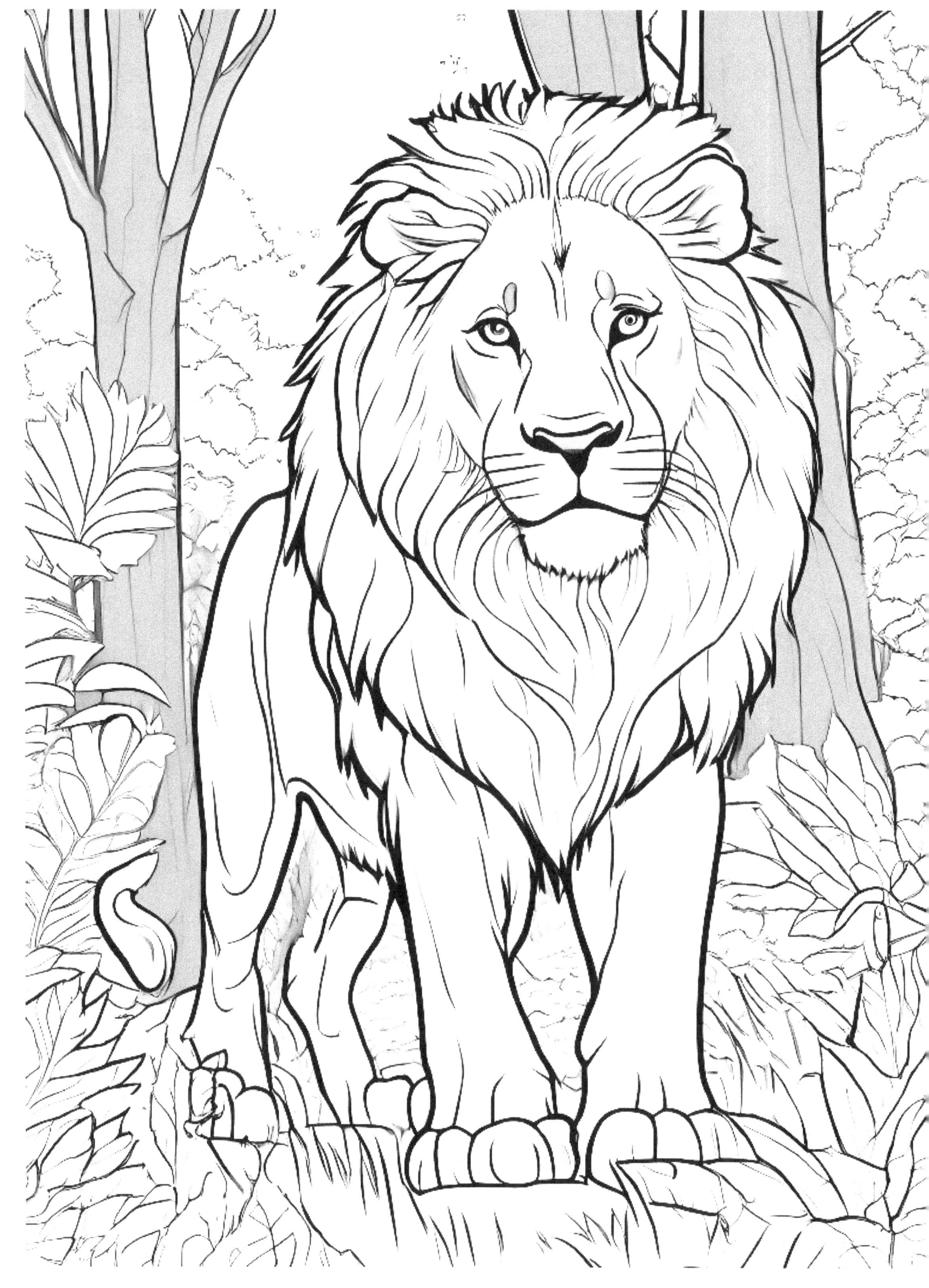

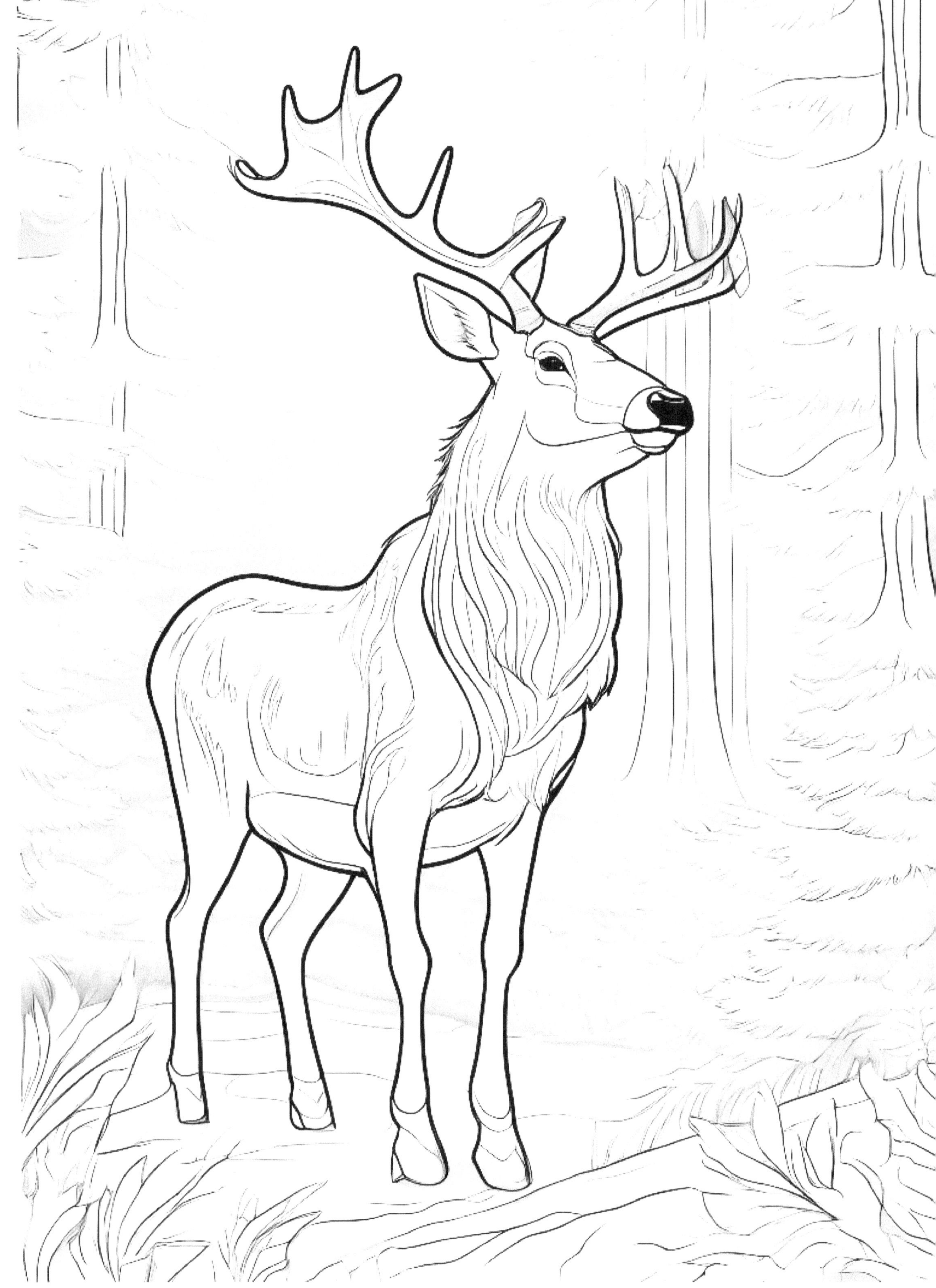

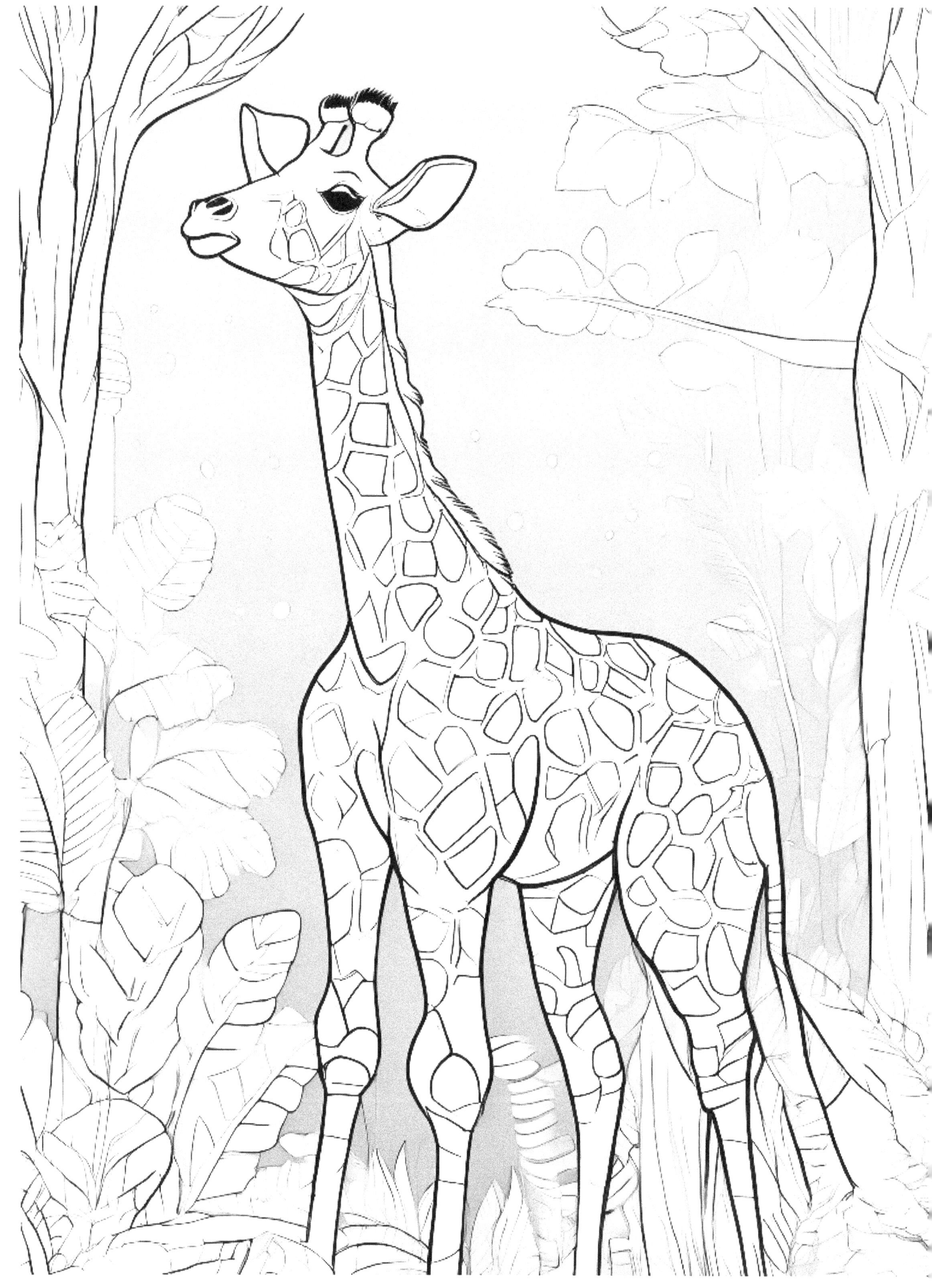

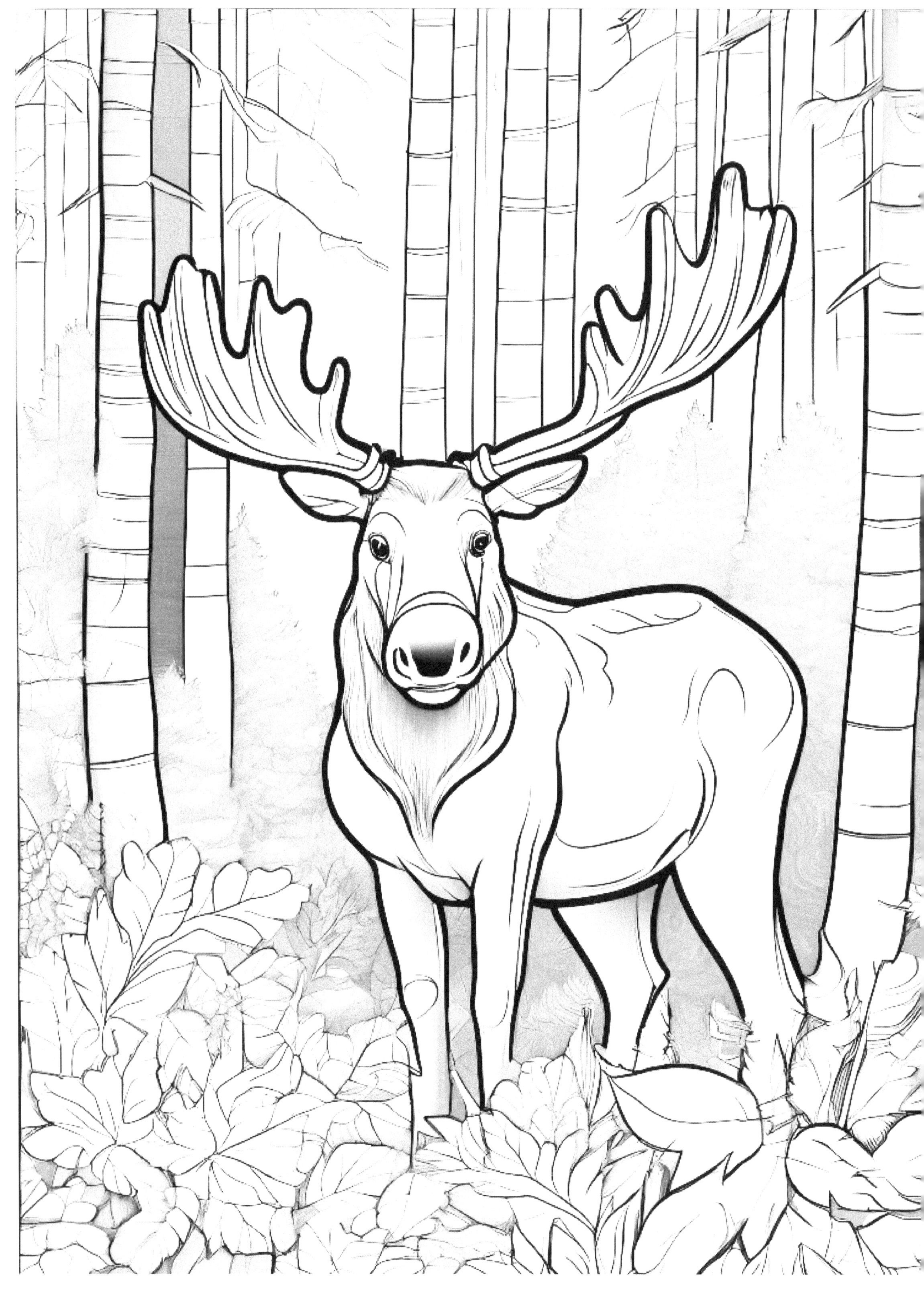

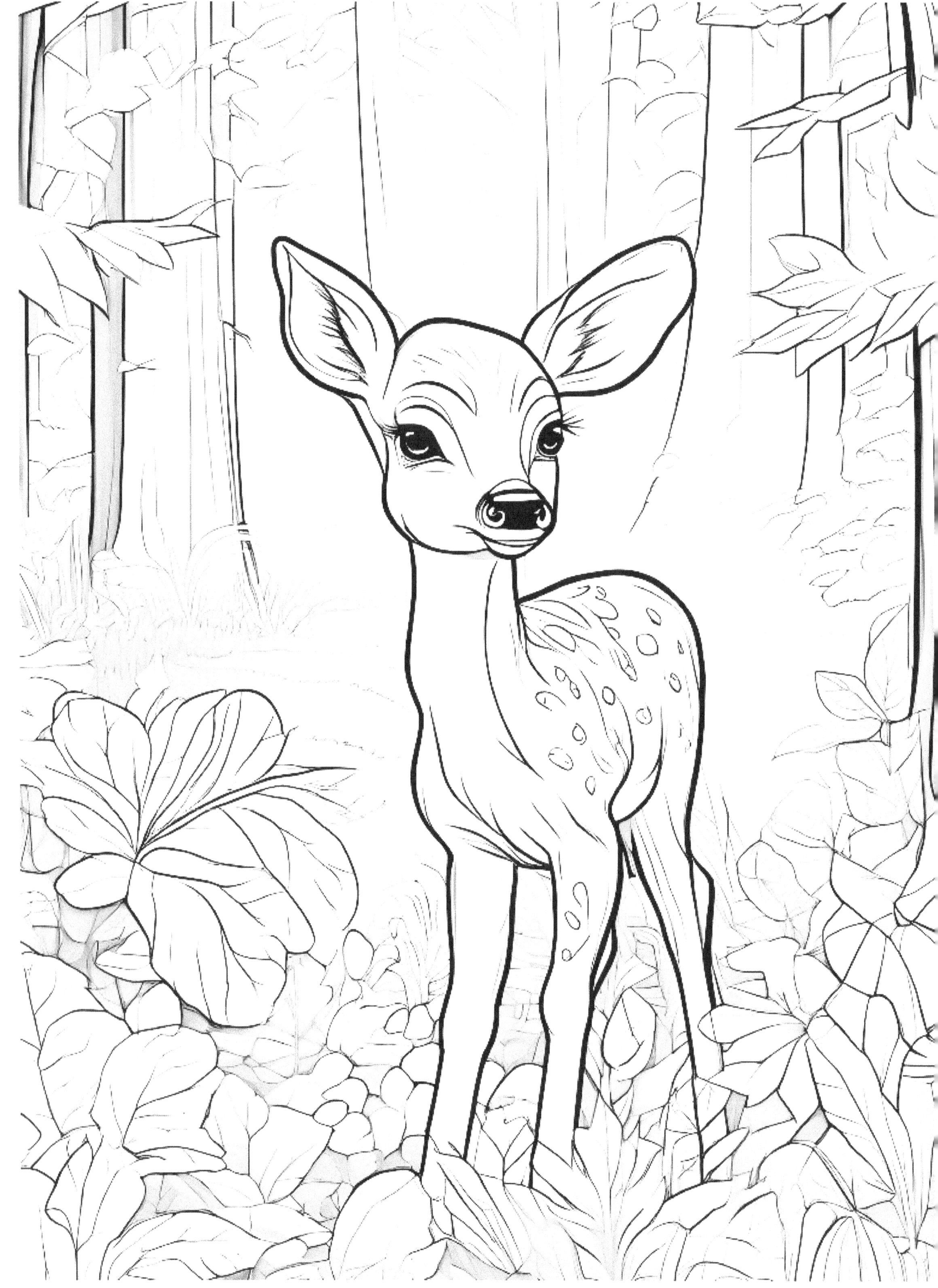

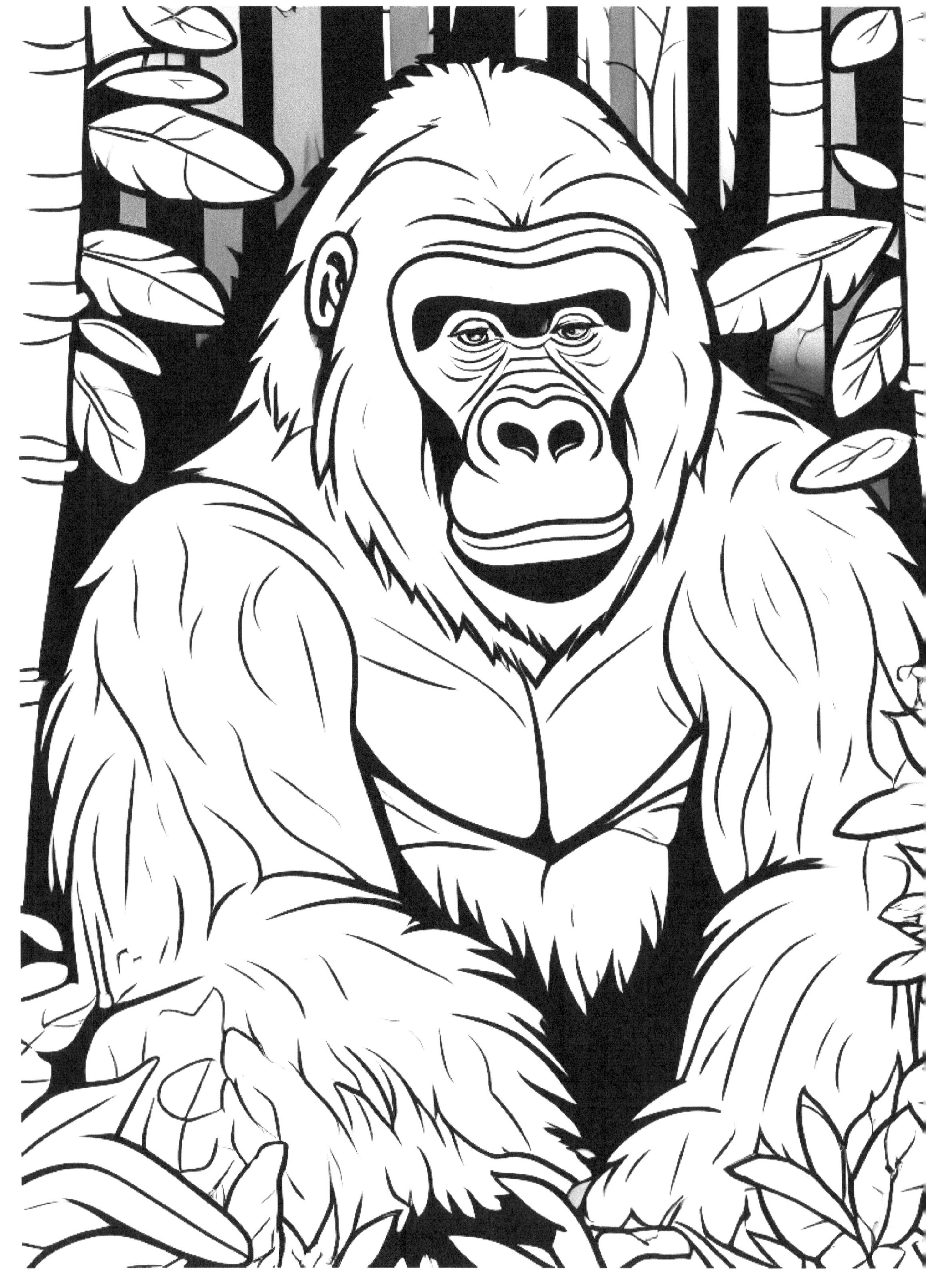

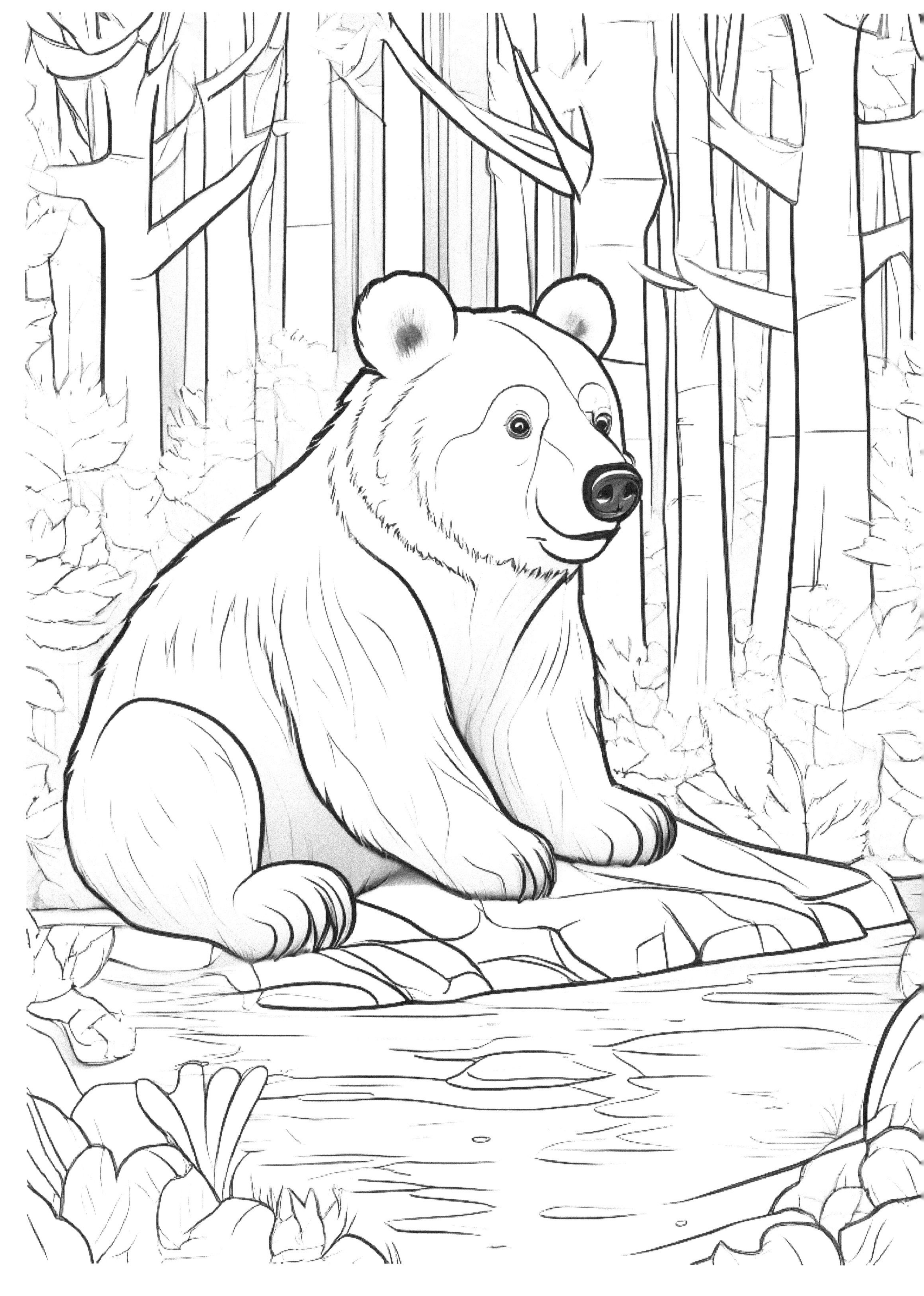

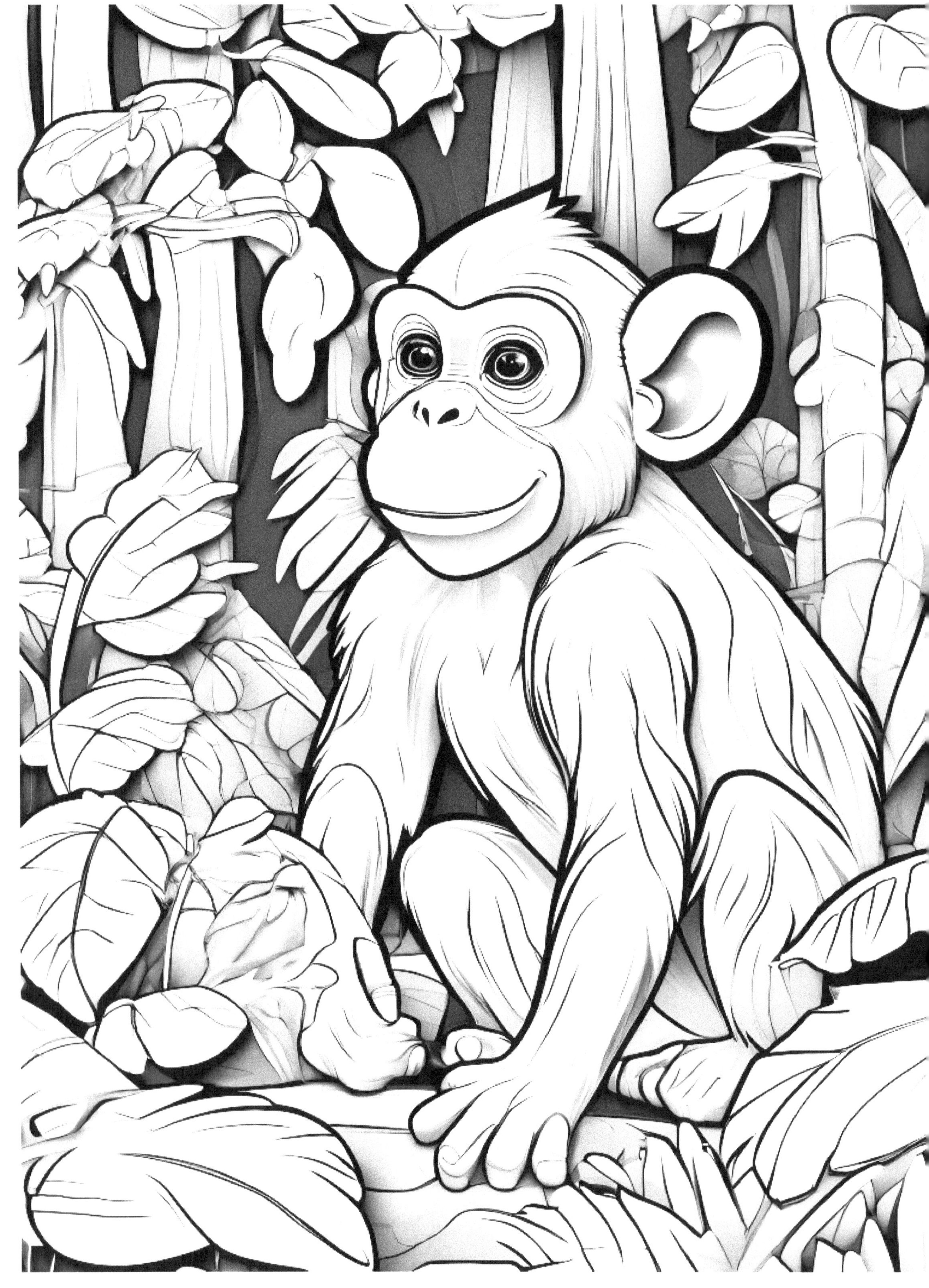

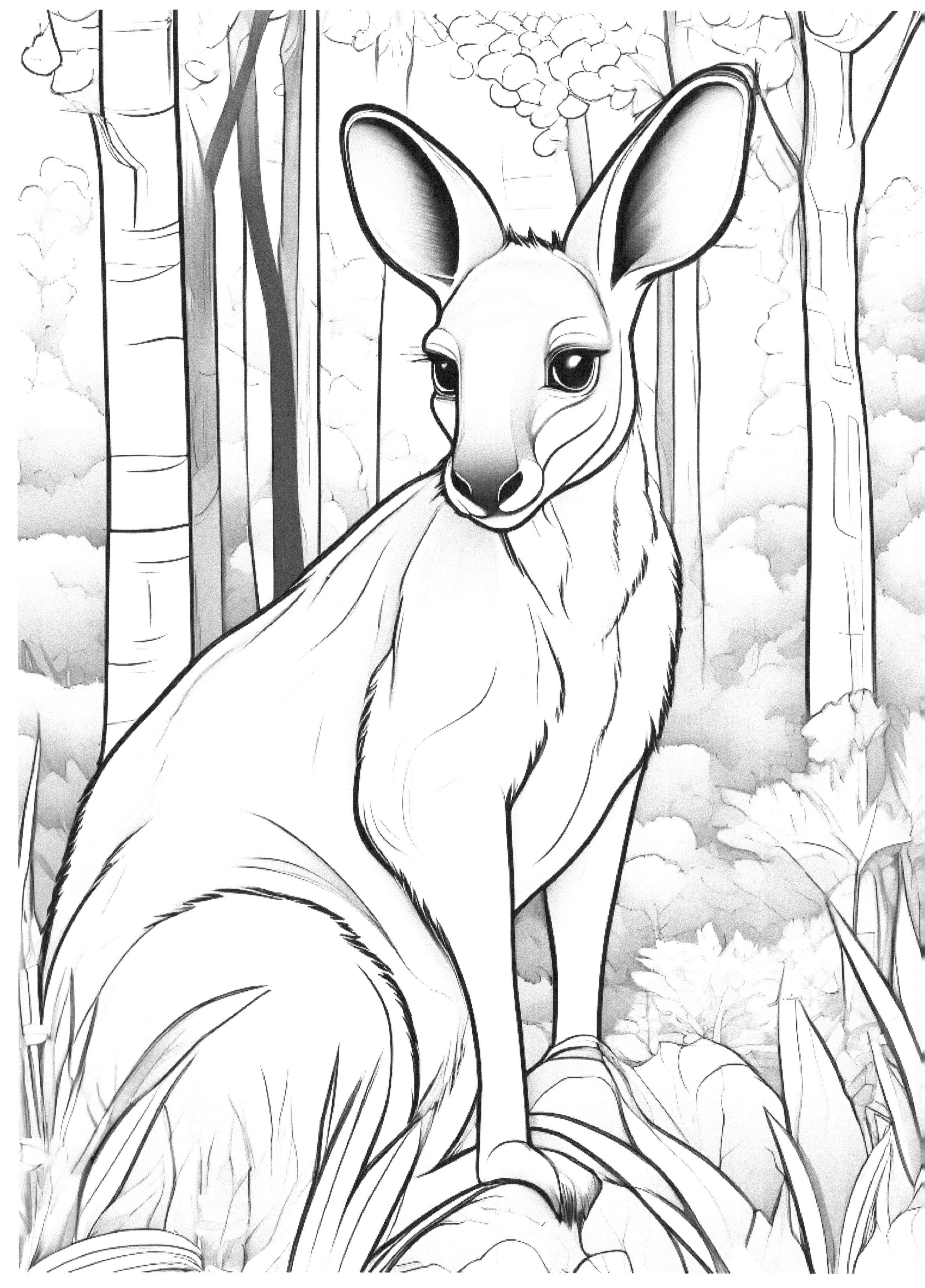

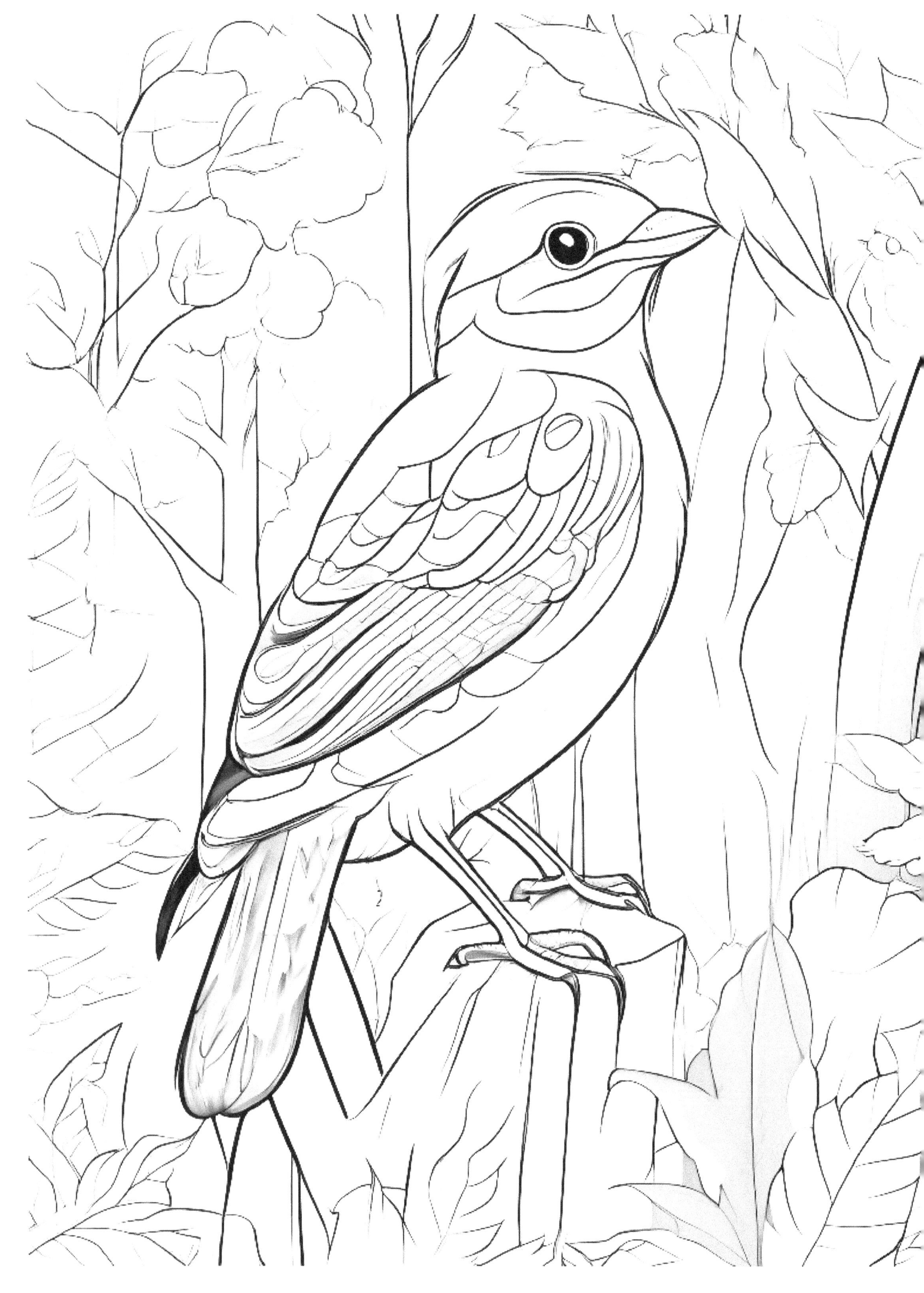

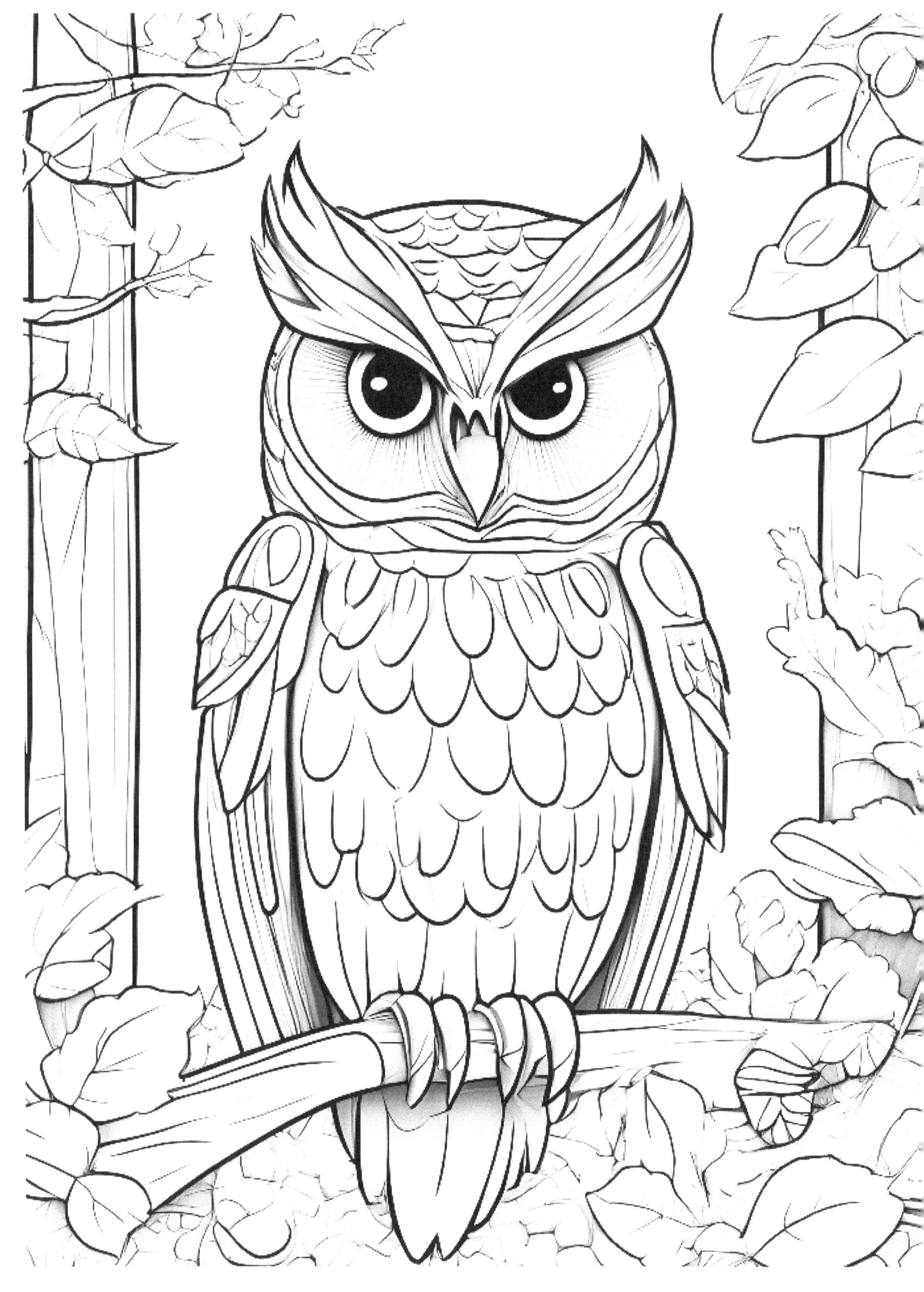

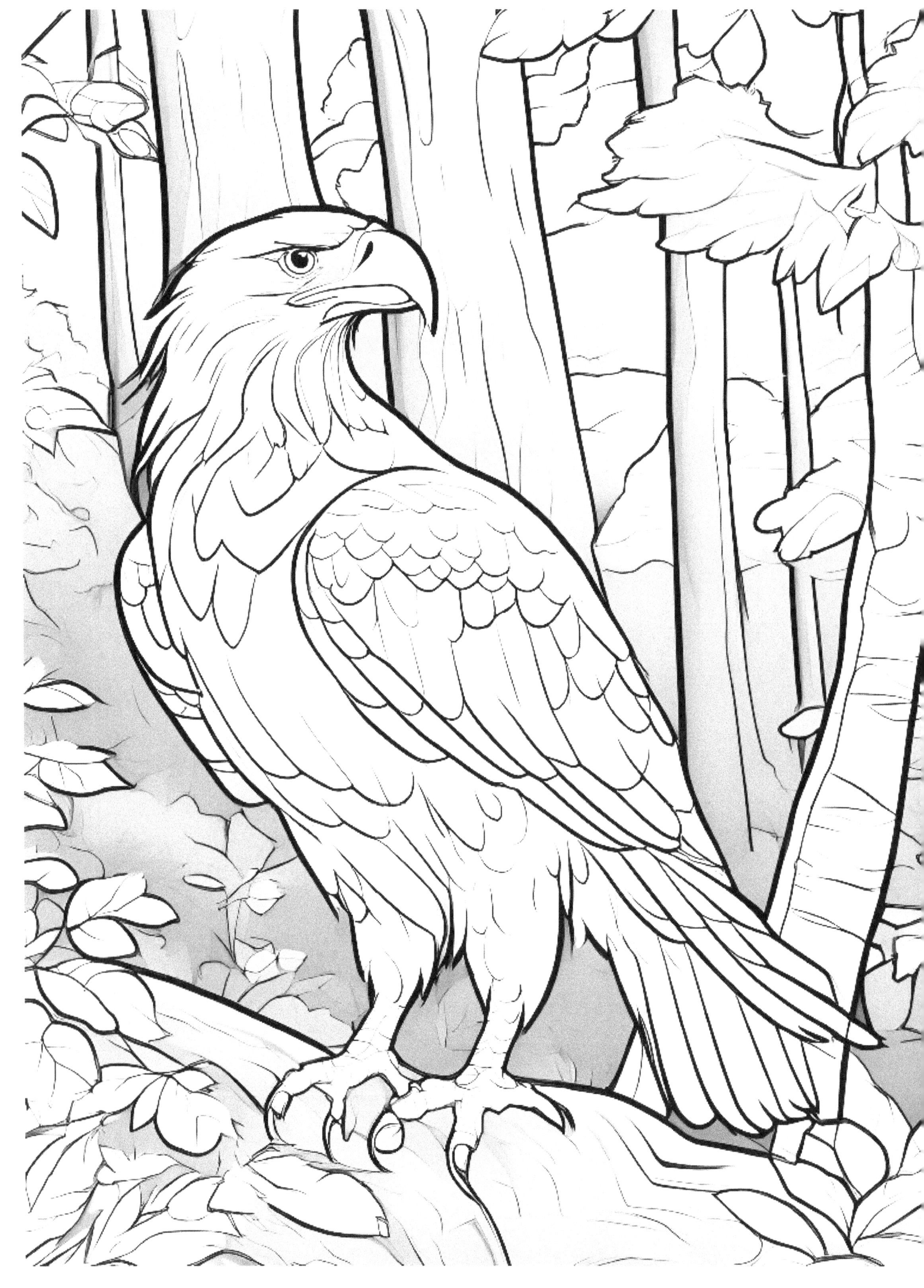

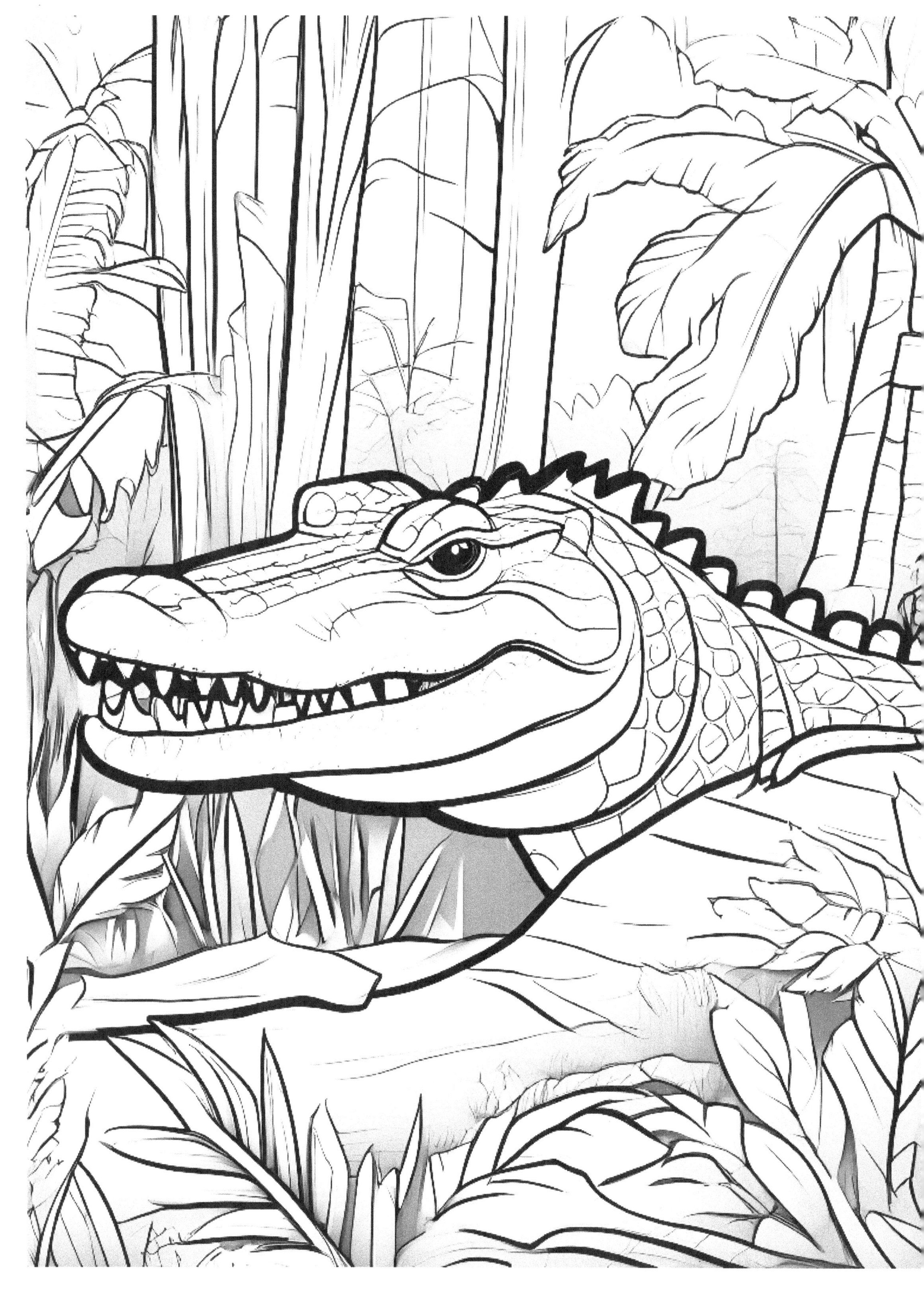

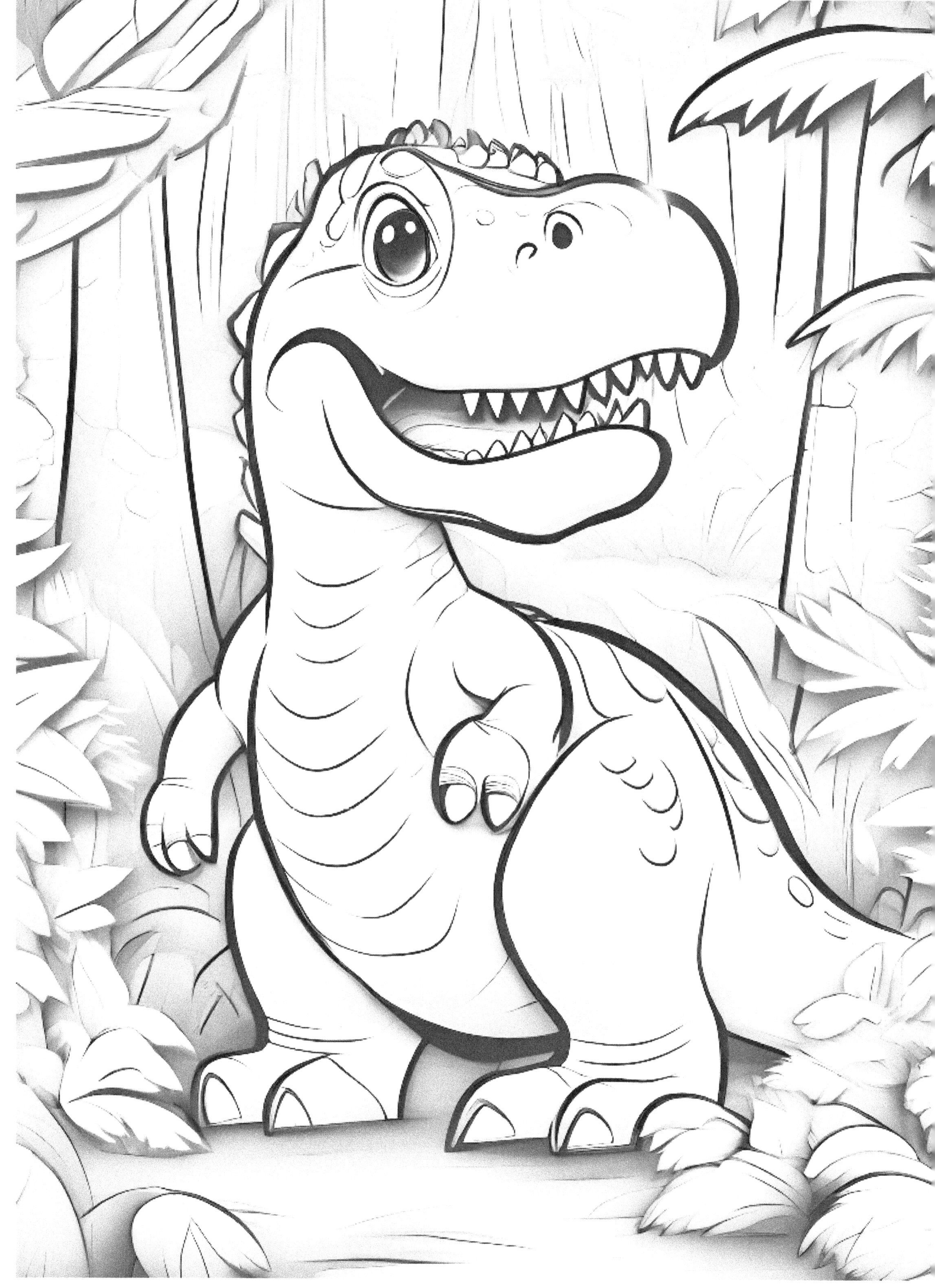

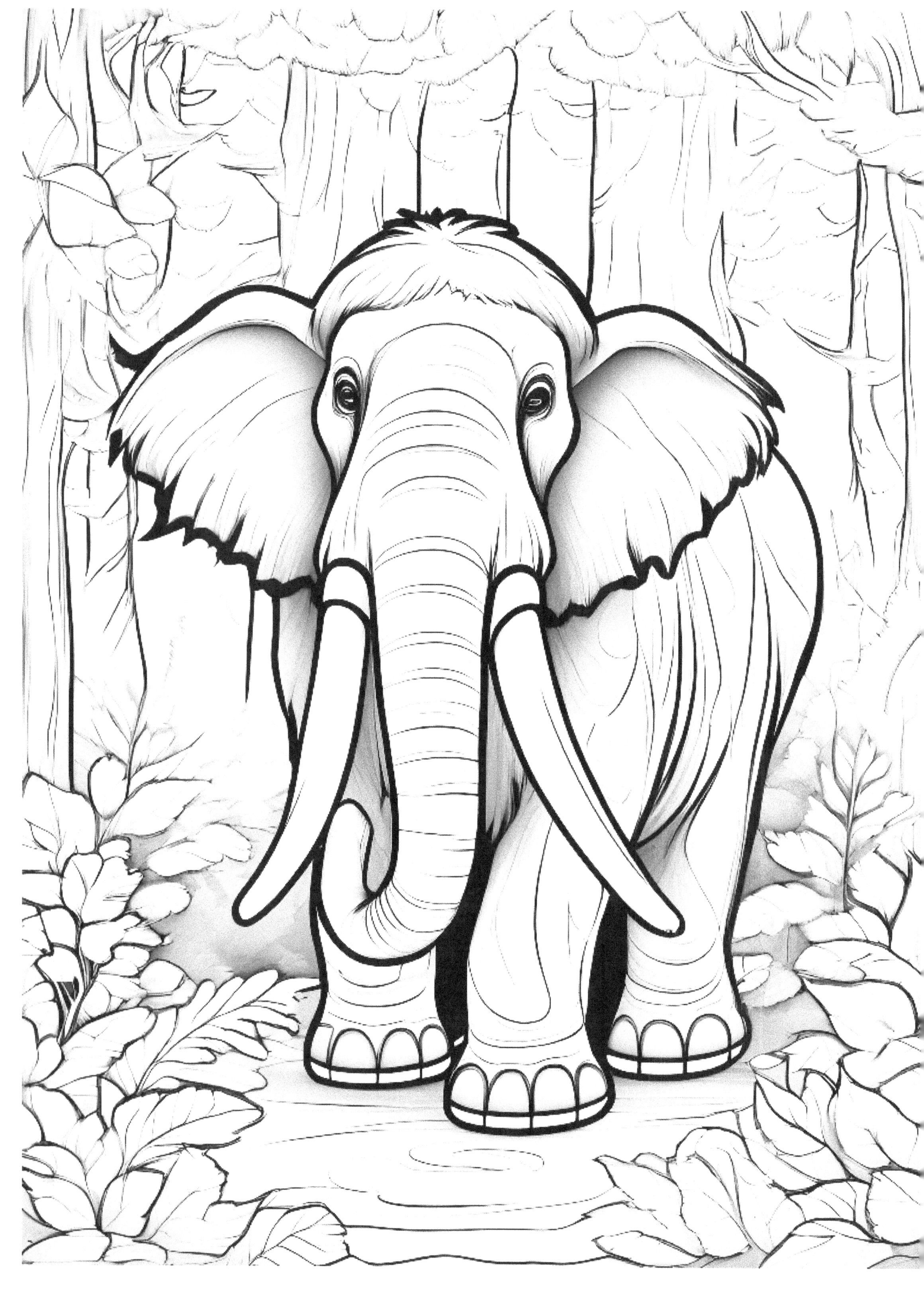

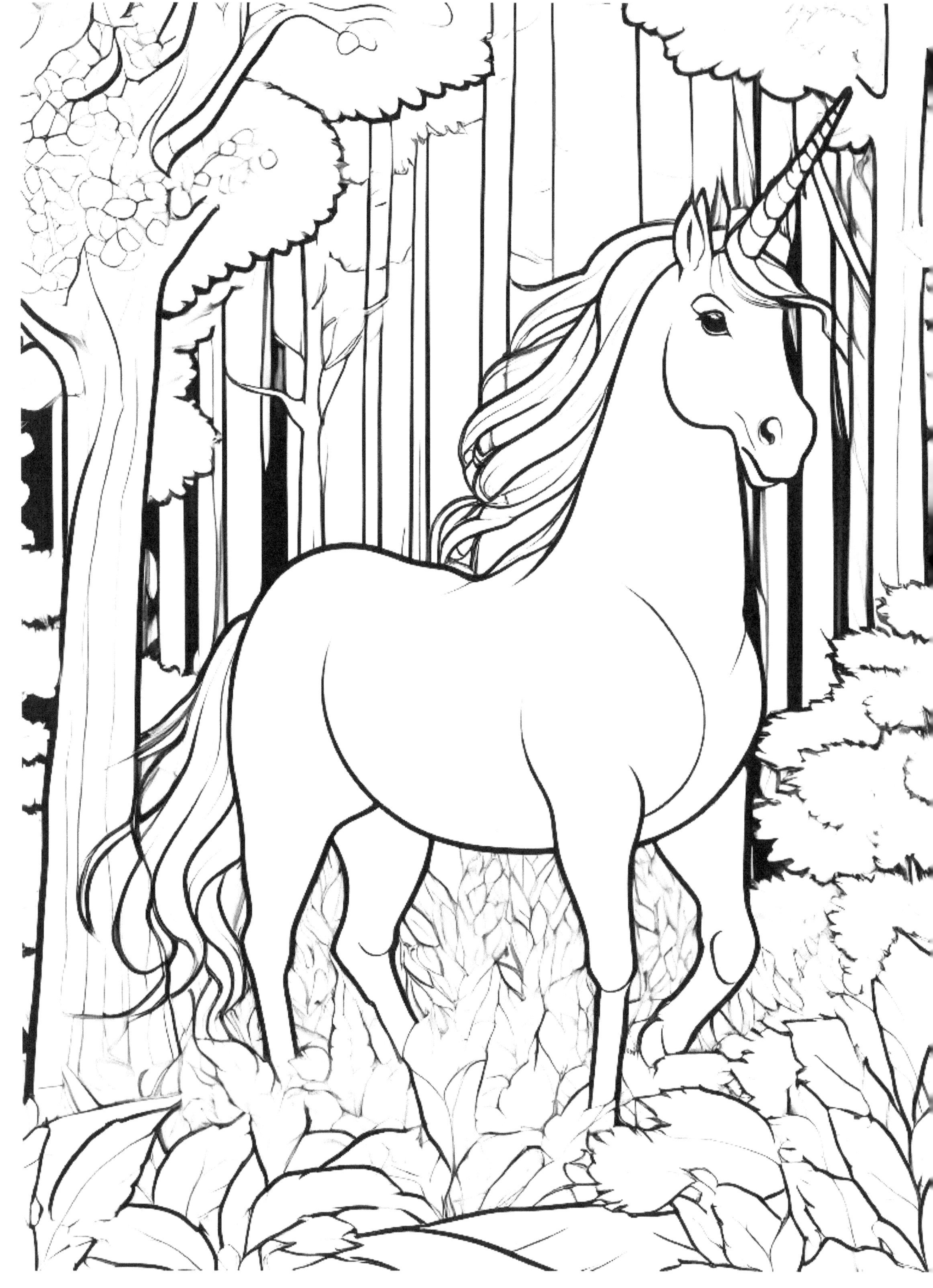